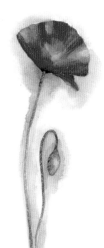

A gift for:

From:

Other books in this series:
For my Granddaughter 365　　Inspiration 365　　Friendship 365　　Yes to life! 365
The Secrets of Happiness 365　For My Sister 365　　365 Calm Days　　365 Happy Days!

Other books by Helen Exley:
The little book of Kindness　　You're a great Son!　　The Resilience book　　For my Friend
Live life to the full　　Being in the Now　　A gem of a Daughter　　Be Happy!

Published in 2011 and 2021 by Helen Exley® LONDON in Great Britain.
Illustrated by Juliette Clarke © Helen Exley Creative Ltd 2011, 2021.
All the words are by Pam Brown © Helen Exley Creative Ltd 2011, 2021.
Selection and arrangement by Helen Exley © Helen Exley Creative Ltd 2011, 2021.

ISBN: 978-1-78485-330-3

12　11　10　9　8　7　6　5　4　3　2　1

Helen Exley® LONDON, 16 Chalk Hill, Watford, Herts WD19 4BG, UK
www.helenexley.com

January 1

Mother –
the most comfortable
word in
the language.

WHAT IS A HELEN EXLEY GIFTBOOK?

Helen Exley Giftbooks cover the most powerful range of all human relationships: love between couples, the bonds with families and between friends. No expense is spared in making sure that each book is as thoughtful and meaningful a gift as it is possible to create: good to give, good to receive. You have the result in your hands. If you have loved it – tell others! There is no power like word-of-mouth recommendation.

January 2

Mothers come in all shapes and sizes.
Calm, timid, roaring, powerful, dull.
Clever, cunning, awkward, unpredictable.
Wonderful.
Splendid.

December 31

You gave me
all I have.
And best of all
you gave me love.

January 3

A mother's love.
A different love.
A unique love that survives all
trials and tribulations.
A love that is the foundation
of every other love.

December 30

Your love
has always wrapped me
round and kept me safe
from harm.

January 4

You have always made me feel wanted, precious, irreplaceable.

December 29

You have been someone with an inexhaustible supply of love. Whatever I've done. Always.

January 5

Thank you for all you have given me.
The gifts of life, of love, of laughter.

December 28

The small astonishments and delights you found for us – remembered now with joy.

January 6

You held me in your arms
when I was small.
And still I feel them round me,
wherever I may be.
Comforting. Encouraging.
Giving me strength.

December 27

Wherever we go – we your family –
we carry the feel and scent and sound of home –
and you at the heart of all our memories.
We are here for you forever, as you are for us.

January 7

You have taught me that love
is the only thing
in life that never runs out.

December 26

You gave me so much –
but the thing that's made
my life rich and good
and worth the living is the thing
I took for granted, and thought
too ordinary to note.
Your love.
Constant and forever.

January 8

You were my beginning. Gave me stars and seas and mountains. Gave me the companionship of living things. Gave me a place – the chance to create, to change, to dream.

December 25

Whenever I ask what you need,
you always say "There's nothing,
really, Darling". But I hope and hope you
need this one gift – my love and my
gratitude for all you've given me.

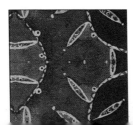

January 9

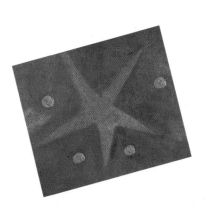

You are always there,
however distant,
constant as the Pole Star.
Unwavering in kindness
and concern – certainty
in an uncertain world.

December 24

Don't worry as a mother if you're short on perfection. Love will do.

January 10

Let me thank you for all the times
that I forgot to thank you –
taking your love, your patience
and forgiveness for granted.

When all else fails
a mother can usually
come up with
a bit of magic.

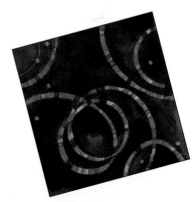

January 11

Thank you for giving me
a childhood
on which I could build a life.

December 22

You gave me a childhood
to treasure and remember.
I hope my children
will have such happy memories.

January 12

You taught me how to learn and how to live.
A special thank-you for a lifetime of love.

December 21

You stood by me
in unhappy times.
And sang when
things went right.

January 13

YOU'RE THE MOTHER
THAT EVERYONE
WOULD LIKE TO HAVE.

December 20

Thank you for always being there
when we most needed you –
a quiet certainty
that gave us strength to find a way.

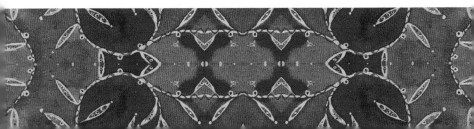

January 14

Wherever you are is home.

December 19

Mothers hold
the world together
when all seems
set on its destruction.

January 15

Whatever I achieve –
you gave me
the courage to begin.

December 18

Hold us safe
in your love –
and we can face
anything.

January 16

Dear Mother…
We are held safe in your love
– and we can face anything.

December 17

They don't build mothers
like you any more.
Head as full of stories as a general store.
Arms as big as branches to shelter
us from harm – and a heart like a winter
stove to keep us snug and warm.
Laughter like a summer gale.
I'm glad that I got you
the day I was born.

January 17

We are bound together
through good days, bad days,
dull days, days of wild excitement
by all that we have shared
together down the years.
Without each other, how drab
our lives would have been.

December 16

Success. Fame. Reward.
Nothing if your
mother does not approve.

January 18

You are the meaning
and the heart of my life.
My warmth.
My comfort. My love.

December 15

Mother.... Most kind.
Most understanding.
Most forgiving and most dear.

January 19

Still I turn to you, as if you were by my side,
and share the moment.
"Look, Mum, look!" As when I was little
and you showed me the world.

December 14

Wherever I go, I feel
you are beside me, sharing all that
I do. Because you taught me
to think and see and do.

January 20

We have shared so many
unexpected joys. So much adventure
and excitement.
So much contentment. So much love.
Without you I would have been
a shadow, a sigh.
A loneliness.

December 13

Mothers live on forever – their tricks of speech and manner, their convictions, superstitions, enthusiasms and abilities. Even their looks. A woman, growing older, suddenly sees that her hands have become the hands that held her own in childhood, that chopped the carrots, dug the garden, stitched the drooping hems.

January 21

Your mother is a constant light,
a warmth, a comfort –
in whatever life brings.

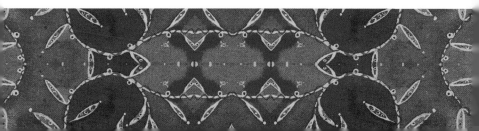

December 12

Thank you for allowing
me to fail, without reproach.
Thank you for your
wild delight when I succeed.

Mothers
come in thousands
of shapes
and sizes – as does love.

December 11

You are the port that we remember – the place
to come home to when we've sailed all the seas,
explored all the islands, had all the adventures.
We may not stay long. Freedom is addictive.
But we'll be back. Again and again.
To our safe haven. To our mother.

January 23

Mothers say, "There's the world, love. Choose yourself some new shades, some new patterns. Make yourself a life."

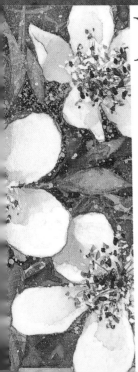

December 10

A MOTHER'S VOICE
STAYS WITH HER
CHILDREN FOREVER.

January 24

Mothers have a way
of picking up the pieces and
making things right again.

December 9

Thank you for all the beginnings.
And for all they've grown to be.
A little of you goes with me
everywhere – gasping with
surprise, smiling with delight.
I turn to you – even
when you are not there.

January 25

Somewhere in the heart
of every one of us is the certainty
this one person is totally their own.
Someone who, when all else fails,
will rescue, heal, comfort,
give all she has.
To her last breath.

December 8

The days pass.
The years pass.
And our lives become
more interwoven –
Until we see
the world through
each other's eyes.

January 26

Thanks to all mothers who say,
"Go ahead and finish them off –
I never liked cherries that much."

December 7

Thanks to all the mothers who made hard times seem good times.

January 27

Thank you
for a thousand
good memories
on which
I've built my life.

December 6

Country or city street,
you were beside me.
Showing me wonders
that others had missed.
Flashing of sun on a tower
of windows. Hammer
of raindrops.
Soaring of wings.

January 28

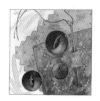  

Mothers.
Multi-skilled.
Multi-talented.
Multi-loved.

December 5

A woman looks at all the things her contemporaries have achieved and feels that she has failed – until she sees her good, kind, sensible, loving children. And knows that that is success enough, for any lifetime.

January 29

Your life has meant
more than you know.
To me and to all
who know you.

December 4

A human being
will remember the kindness
of their Mother's hands,
when all else has faded.

January 30

I know you're
always there for me.
But never forget,
I'm here for you.

December 3

You have been the light
at the end of the tunnel,
the handhold on the cliff-face,
the path through the thicket.
You have been certainty when
all seemed chaos.

January 31

We find safety in our mothers' arms from the very first. And always will.

December 2

Every loving mother has a home full
of kitsch. Gifts to be treasured.
Necklaces you made as a child.
Popeyed crinoline ladies.
Saucer-eyed poodles. Rusting cow bells.
Love made visible.

February 1

Thank you for our beginnings –
the best there could ever be.

December 1

My extraordinary mother –
giving us all we needed, and
never letting us know the cost in time
and effort, the sacrifice of dreams.

February 2

We are linked
to home by invisible,
unbreakable threads –
forever.

November 30

Forget about being
the Perfect Mother –
we love you
as you are.

February 3

You swung me high.
You spun me round.
You caught me on the slide.
You found me bread
to feed the ducks.
And made the park
a magic place to be.

November 29

Wh en we are young, mother is there,
as certain as the sun rising – someone to
tidy up after us, feed us, clothe us, sort out our
problems, nag us, love us. Not a human being.
One of a totally different species. Mothers.
Suddenly we see her as a contemporary –
a person in her own right. Someone to share
with, someone to question. The person
who has shared our lifetime. The person who
taught us how to love.

February 4

Thank you for leaving us our secrets –
even though you knew them.
For never saying "I told you so"–
although you had. For never interfering –
though somehow things were put to rights.

November 28

In times of trouble I turn to you.
And in times of joy, achievement, wonder.
You are part of all I do and am.

February 5

Thank you for
leaving me to decide
when to stand my ground
and when
to walk away.

November 27

MOTHERS HOLD THE WORLD TOGETHER.
NO MOTHERS. NO WORLD.

February 6

What's a shopping expedition
without you to share it?
To giggle over the ridiculous,
to exclaim at the magnificent,
to hold each other back
– or egg each other on.

November 26

To be a mother...
To live in utter poverty,
to create meals from
almost nothing,
to keep the children clothed and safe,
to bring laughter into dreariness,
to keep hope alive.

In an uncertain world
you are my certainty.

November 25

Thank you for the kitten.
The bike. The stunt kite.
The party dress. Things I longed for
– and that you couldn't really afford
– but found a way to give me.
By going without yourself.

February 8

Thank you for putting my doll's eyes back in their sockets. For staying up all night to make me a clown's costume for the play I'd forgotten to mention. For making me a ballet birthday cake. For getting me a kitten.
For all the treats and surprises and marvels and magic that you brought to my childhood.

November 24

Mothers never die.
They set up home in their children's hearts
and live there forever and forever.

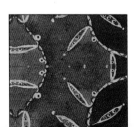

February 9

Where ballet, drama, tennis,
football are concerned,
mothers can be at all of them at once.

A MOTHER
IS ALWAYS IN DANGER
OF MEETING HERSELF
COMING BACK.

November 23

Nightmare in the darkness, waking in a fright.
My mother in her dressing gown,
with a candle. Not a sign of giants.
Not a bear in sight.
Sits there beside me,
talking very softly.
Kissing me goodnight.
And everything all right.

February 10

The important things
you taught me
were given so quietly
I never saw the giving.

November 22

We were so caught up in being young we did not see your sacrifice, your long endurance, your courage, or your weariness. It did not occur to us to thank you. But take it now – our lifetime's love – the too-long-hoarded gratitude.

February 11

Mothers have been respected,
and admired all through time.
But the price is unimaginably high.

November 21

Thank you for turning up
for every Parents' Evening.
And the Bazaars.
And the Recorder Concerts.
And the School Plays.
Oh – and for driving me
wherever, I needed to be.

February 12

Your life is so full – and yet I know that,
always, always, there is room for me.

November 20

When a child has reached new heights
of sheer impossibility
and a mother is tempted to cut and run
– that is the moment when,
overnight, without warning,
she becomes a companion and a friend.

February 13

Sometimes the greatest comfort is
to return to the nest and be a little child again.
Hot-water bottles, tea and sympathy.

November 19

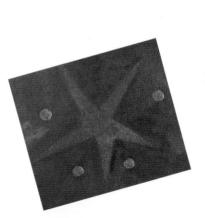

Mothers ask
only one thing
for their children.
That they should
be happy.

February 14

Thank you
for the laughter, the cuddles.
The chases. The fun. Thank you
for so much happiness.
So much tenderness.
So much love.

November 18

All my life
your love will
wrap around me and
give me comfort
in the darkest days.

February 15

Dear Mothers:

You are our own dear, complicated, aggravating mothers. Clever or muddle-headed — or both together. Tidy or chaotic. Quiet or roaring ones. The ones we need to feel ourselves complete. There may be a perfect mother somewhere. But we prefer our own.

November 17

You put up with me through all
the Nothing Days – when nothing made sense,
nothing was worth bothering about.
You went on believing that one day
I'd come out of the fog and find the sun again.
And I did.

February 16

I feel your arms
holding me safe,
even with a thousand
miles between us.

November 16

Thank you for giving me
all that I needed when I was young –
including wonderful, amazing,
hilarious fun.

February 17

You have given so much of yourself –
to my friends, relations, strangers.
So quietly.
But we know.
And we will always remember.

November 15

We who have mothers,
who have loved us, cared for us,
helped us to live with hopeful
and courageous hearts –
we are the most fortunate of men
and women.

February 18

The wisest, kindest, most modern and informed
parent sometimes thinks wistfully
of sitting-in-the-corner-with-face-to-the-wall.
And silence.

November 14

A good mother will endure
and hope when
everyone else has turned away.

February 19

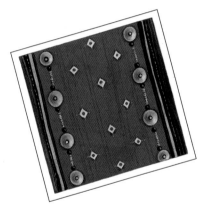

Mothers
clear up the messes
mankind creates.

November 13

Thank you for letting me lick
the cake-mix bowl. For dribbling my
name in syrup on my porridge.
For cutting tomatoes into stars.
For making food an adventure.
For working a little homely magic.

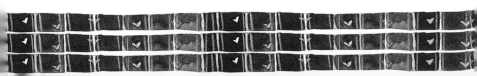

February 20

I only knew the happiness
of your love and the certainty
of your care.

November 12

Thank you for the love that has outlasted every trial and trouble.

February 21

Mothers...

Mother in an apron.
Mother in a city street.
Mother in a sari. Mother in dungarees.
Mother in an academic gown.
But always your mother at heart.

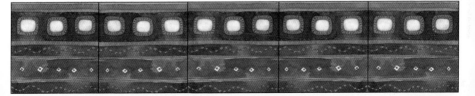

November 11

I don't know how you did it
– but I know
I could never have survived
without you.
I hope when I have children
I can do the same.

February 22

"See, no goblins in the cupboard,
no dragons underneath the bed.
Sleep now," you said.
"Safe and sound till morning – I'm never far away."
And so I drifted into sleep,
wrapped in your love.

All mothers are very useful.
At giving cues. At hearing verse.
At checking homework.
Though, with mathematics, you're
mostly on your own.

February 23

Sorry for temper, defiance, laziness, contrariness.
Spite. Noise and untidiness. Stupidity
and showing off. You stood your ground.
You stood by me. How, I am not too sure.
But thank you.

November 9

When it comes down to it, a mother
is just another woman.
The only difference being that she is expected
to perform miracles on a regular basis.

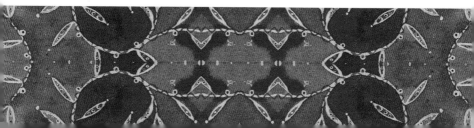

February 24

The path of a mother is marked
by abandoned cups of tea.

Mothers dream
of a good night's sleep
and a cup of tea
that is not stone cold.

November 8

Any mother could run a business empire.
Every day she faces the making of a hundred
decisions – coping with a hundred problems.
They are courageous and determined –
and possessed of a genius for lateral thought.
Mothers are miracles.

February 25

Mothers ask little of you:
Say please and thank you.
Wear mended underwear.
Wash the back of your neck.
Eat nicely.
It is imprinted indelibly
on the mind and heart
and soul.
Forever.

November 7

Mothers are the people who comfort you in the worst times with the same voice they used when you were two. And it works.

February 26

When it's sorrow
beyond keeping,
phone home.

November 6

THE CERTAINTY OF A MOTHER'S LOVE
CAN SUSTAIN ONE THROUGH A LIFETIME.

February 27

Mother, I am myself. I make my own decisions.
I live my own life. And yet.
I make a gesture – and it is yours.
I laugh – and it is your laughter.
I hold something to be true – and it is a truth you taught me.
I am myself. But I am of your making. As you were
of your mother's.
We take and we give.
A hundred years from now
a little girl will smile just as you smile today.

November 5

A mother gives us the stars,
sunlight, trees and mountains,
lakes and waterfalls –
friendship and love and the chance
to do a thousand things.

February 28/29

The nearest thing
to magic
that we have
is a mother.

November 4

You
LIGHT UP
OUR
LIVES.

March 1

With the approach of Mother's Day,
the mob of wild-eyed daughters
progressing from shop to shop
are all looking for cards
that just say
"Thank you.
I love you".

November 3

A mother can move from point A to point B
at the speed of light, in pitch darkness
and nine tenths asleep, evading the dog,
the rocking horse and a pair of roller skates –
to deal with any misery or terror.

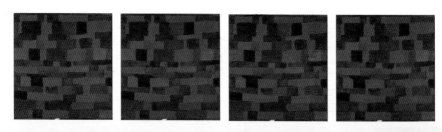

March 2

A wise and loving mother
is the best beginning.

November 2

A mother in later years
is always astounded
at the things her children
have forgiven.

You are my lightship,
my candle in the window.
You keep me on course.

Styles change
down the centuries.
But mothers' hearts
are constant.

Mothers hold their families
together against all odds.

October 31

When I am afraid I still reach out to you,
however far I am from you.
And know I'll feel you take my hand
and steady me, and give me comfort.

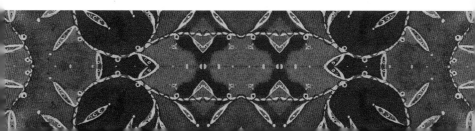

March 5

In a changing world
you are our certainty.

October 30

 ${\rm A}$ woman will take on almost any job, whatever her qualifications – char, kitchen hand, chief executive officer – to feed her children.

March 6

Mothers
are the background
to all our lives.

October 29

I look back today and remember
how you bent down and showed me miracles.
A speck of purple at a flower's heart,
the pollen-dusted fur of a honeybee,
and a bird's bright eye.
Thank you.

A defensive mother tiger has nothing on a human mother confronted by someone she feels endangers her children.

You never gave up on me, however foolish I was. Your belief steadied, reassured, encouraged me – and gave me the hope and courage to find a better way.

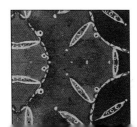

March 8

Let me tell you now how much I love you, how much you mean to me, how much you have always meant to me. Let me thank you now for all the joys we've shared, for all you've given me, for all your help and patience.

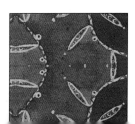

October 27

Not since mankind began
has there been another mother
quite like you.
Each one is unique.
Each loved in a special way.
For me no one else will do.
For me you are my dearest friend.
My dearest mother, forever.

March 9

There are times when only your mother will do.

October 26

You are our reassurance that
goodness still exists.
And patience, kindness, love.

March 10

Only now do we begin to understand
all that you sacrificed for us.
All you endured. All you forgave.
Take my thanks, belated, inadequate.
Take my love forever.

October 25

Thank heavens for the mothers of children
struggling against terrible difficulties.
Mothers who, with courage and determination,
patience and enduring love,
go on doing all they can. Who go on hoping.

March 11

A mother juggles children, pets, husband, bills, shopping, cooking, cleaning, doctor, dentist and vet visits, sudden emergencies, clubs, parties and swimming lessons with apparent ease. And no sleep.

October 24

You saw us through the bad times
– you shared our good times.

March 12

Mother love
can be the greatest
force in nature.

October 23

You gave me the love
and certainty
that I can cope everywhere.

March 13

Thank you for all the moppings-up, the dustings-down, the washings and the bandagings.

Thanks to all the mothers
who chopped up the best things
in their wardrobe to make us
a party frock overnight, who sang us
home in the rain, who tried their
hand at algebra,
who shared our chickenpox.

March 14

Poor mothers!
Somehow or other the idea has grown
that they aren't bothered
by sick and poo and nits and blood
and snot.

October 21

Thank you for the little things –
a pat in passing, a snuggle, a hug.
A friendly wink, a smile, a hand clasp.
A cup of tea, buttered toast.
An egg and dippits. A rose in a milk bottle.
The little things that make my life possible.

March 15

For your constancy and care when I was small.
For your gentleness when I was sick.
For your patience and forgiveness when
I behaved so badly. For your sittings-up until
my key was in the door. For your strength
and your encouragement when I was in distress.
For your faith in me.
Your love for me. For always being there for me.
With thanks, my dear and lovely mother.

October 20

You have taken most
ordinary things and made
of them astonishments.
Thank you for the magic
of childhood.

March 16

Mothers can create
a festival from nothing.

October 19

Whatever troubles come between a mother
and her children – they are one
in blood and bone and mind and heart.

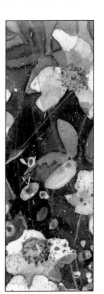

Mothers forgive
when no one else will.

October 18

You taught us kindness,
patience, empathy.
Where we have failed it's been our fault.
When we have succeeded
the credit is all yours.

March 18

Mothers mix a brew
of scents. Polish, talcum
powder and baked apples.
Oranges and lilac.
Burnt toast. Clean linen.
It meets us at the door.
Warm. Safe. Home.

October 17

Mothers are inclined to sigh over the past –
misunderstandings, wrong decisions,
undeserved scoldings.
And are astonished to discover that their
children have set all that aside, long since –
and remember their childhood with joy.

March 19

So PROUD. Mothers need to be dignified when a child has some success – but end up telling all their friends and relatives.

October 16

A MOTHER IS MORE
THAN A FRIEND.
SHE IS A PART OF YOU
FOREVER.

March 20

Mothers are more necessary
than anything else in one's life.

October 15

Thank you for magical times...
The splendid times, the rampaging
times, the times of happy lunacy.
The pillow fight that ended
in a storm of feathers. Shoes were
unpolished. Dinners were erratic.
But we had magic.
And that has outlasted everything.

March 21

Thank you for lending me your earrings,
your perfume, your shoes, your tights.
Even though you didn't know you did!

October 14

A MOTHER BELIEVES
THAT IF SHE CAN STAND
SHE CAN COPE.

March 22

The trip when it rained, the concert
that went on too long, the zoo visit
when most of the animals were hidden
in piles of straw –
seemed failures at the time.
But will be remembered
in loving detail by the children
thirty years on.

October 13

You seem always so sure,
so confident that I will come through.
But I know how often you have lain awake,
living through everything I suffer.

March 23

No one looks as lonely as your mother before she sees you coming up the platform.

October 12

Thank you
for all those happy,
happy days –
and for all that I am,
and hope for.

March 24

Something stupendous
has happened?
Time to celebrate?
But first, time to contact
your mother.

October 11

In a really tight spot
even the great adventurer
wants his mother.

March 25

You were there – close by when
I was very small and still within reach,
however far time and circumstance have
divided us. I have only to reach for you –
and you are there.

October 10

Thank you, for being eager to praise
me whenever I'd done something well
and loving and encouraging me whenever
I had failed completely.

March 26

You were the one who banished the shapes that haunt the dark of childhood, who helped me find courage when I needed it.

Whatever goes wrong –
I can always say
"At any rate, my mother loves me!"

March 27

You loved me.
Still love me.
And I love you back.
Thank you for being
my dear mother.

October 8

Mothers wonder why
Nature did not fit children
with noise suppressors.

March 28

You are more than our mother.
Because you are you.

October 7

Thank you for reading all of the children's books
with all the voices
– teaching me to dance a riotous polka....
A hundred rhymes, a hundred stories,
a hundred songs.

March 29

You are a mother among mothers – the makers of the world. Wealth or poverty have no part in it, or race or creed or place or time. You weave the generations. Your love has been learned for all those who went before you – it is your gift to all who are to come. Your children carry it.

October 6

MOTHERS
FORGIVE
AND FORGET.

March 30

Of all the mothers
in the world
how wonderful that
you are mine.

October 5

To all the mothers
who fashioned presents
out of nothing.
Who conjured excitement
and delight from
ordinary things.
Thank you forever.

March 31

With a loving, understanding mother
behind you, you will have
the courage to make a good life.

October 4

The family disperses. University.
A voyage round the world.
The Big City. But mother is the central
point about which they turn.

April 1

Mothers can replace Teddys ears, conduct funeral services over dead mice, grow beans in blotting paper, stretch the lunch to three more places, sort out bullies, unblock the drains and cure just about everything with a hug.

October 3

You must resign yourself.
Your mother is going to go on
giving you advice, worrying
about your health and your decisions
until you are older
than she is today.

April 2

A mother…
is a lady who can do a dozen
things at once –
and still find time to kiss
a bruised knee better.

October 2

Mothers can and must
be capable of being in two places at once.

Who can get one child to an exam,
another to piano lessons
and another to her tennis tournament
all at the same time?
A mother can.

April 3

Time and distance mean very little
to mothers and daughters who love each other.
They can always find a way to reach out
to each other, comfort each other,
give each other courage.

October 1

A mother is a very ordinary woman
who suddenly, astoundingly, finds herself able
to diagnose rubella, replace loose
doll's eyes, mend a bike,
cook for twenty, put in zips,
sew up a split
while the taxi's waiting.

April 4

You never realise how much your mother loves you till you explore the attic and find every letter you ever sent her, every finger painting, clay pot, bead necklace, paper lace Mother's Day card and school report since day one.

September 30

Mothers come in all shapes and sizes –
and you are exactly the one
that I would have chosen if I had had my pick.

April 5

You are a part of
everything we do.
You are the heartbeat
of the family.

September 29

However different we are.
However we disagree.
One thing we share.
Our love holds us together.

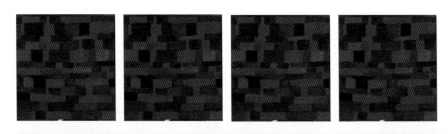

April 6

Thank you
for all lovely things.
And wonder.
And happiness.

September 28

We took you for granted –
but that was only because we were so certain
of your caring, your patience, your love,
your forgiveness.
We scarcely saw you as a person then –
you were simply our mother,
the sure and certain core of our lives.

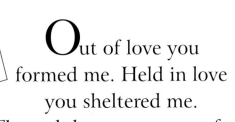

Out of love you
formed me. Held in love
you sheltered me.
Through love you set me free.
How could I do anything but love
you in return.

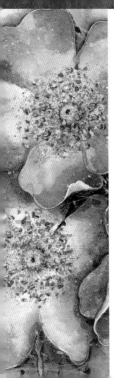

September 27

You are no different now
to us, your children,
than when we scrambled
onto your knees
and nuzzled in your hair
for comfort.

April 8

We learn at our mother's knee to love and trust, to rejoice in life and to go forward with confidence and hope.

September 26

The average family household
is held together with sellotape,
string, glue, wire,
ingenuity and desperation.
Poor Mum!

You have made a home
for us in the midst
of the world's tumult –
a place of certainty,
a place of welcome.

September 25

You turned hard times
into adventures.
Concocted meals from strange
ingredients.
Made birthdays magic.
Thank you. Always.

April 10

Mothers are fuelled by tea and sticky kisses.

September 24

Mothers should repeat, very firmly,
their own names. The name that they had
before they were wives or mothers. The name of
the skilled, independent woman with a multitude
of interests that they once were.
And are. And are. And are.

April 11

The link between
mother and child
is endlessly elastic.

September 23

Out of poverty,
out of wretchedness
mothers have made homes
that their children
will remember with love,
and gratitude.

April 12

To others we are simply pebbles
on the beaches of existence.
But our mothers know every subtlety
of difference – and that none
of us are identical, or commonplace.

September 22

Out of the slums, the wilderness, come doctors and teachers, engineers and farmers. Beginning their lives with nothing – given their opportunities, their victories, by their mothers. At a cost beyond our comprehension. But with joy and pride and love.

April 13

A mother informed that you are
unexpectedly to take the lead
in the school play tomorrow,
will have your costume made by dawn.

September 21

You took all the ordinary
things of every day
and made me feel special.

April 14

When it comes
to the crunch,
the bravest, wisest,
most sophisticated people
call for their mothers.

September 20

Mothers know whose turn it is to lick out the cake-mix bowl. They know when it's a real stomach-ache and when it's physics morning. They know the difference between a bit of fantasizing and a straight lie; between "I Must Have" and "I Want".

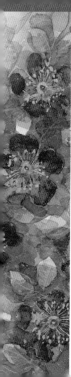

April 15

Whether they realise it or not
a mother and her child
are still entangled, even into age –
and one's pain and joy
lives in the other's heart.

September 19

A silk thread
is stronger than
a thread of steel.
The thread of maternal love
is stronger by far
than either.

April 16

Thank you for wanting me, all of me,
and not counting up my successes
and my mistakes and marking me accordingly.

September 18

Thank you for the kissings
and the scoldings,
the stories and the surprises.
I'll never forget them. Ever.

April 17

Thank you for having the ability to send love and understanding and comfort down the telephone.

September 17

The modern Western mother
has an impossible timetable,
endless appointments,
consultations, assessments,
financial decisions.
And still finds
time for a fairy story.

April 18

There are huggy, kissy mothers –
and smiley, talking mothers.
And sometimes a mother
who combines it all. Mine.

September 16

A surgeon and a dancer
in earnest conversation.
Ethics? Artistry? Historical significance? No.
Their kids.

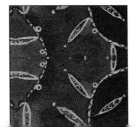

April 19

It is the small things that can shake the head with longing for the past. A white hyacinth set on the table by my sick bed. The solemn fitting of my first boots. A party outfit you sewed between dusk and dawn. Thank you for it all... the secret wisdom and the gifts of love.

September 15

Mothers never
get the chocolate biscuit.

April 20

We hold you in our hearts, wherever life may take us – for we were created from all you are. However much we have taken, however much we have let go, however much we have reshaped and changed, you are our beginning. You are the hallmark of our minds, our hearts, our substance.

September 14

For us, you are our touchstone – the standard by which we judge the value of our lives.

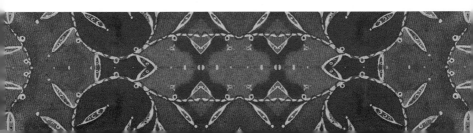

April 21

Thank you for making
having-to-make-do a game.
Thank you for making
adventures out of small events.
Astonishments. Delights.

September 13

Any respectable mother can
at a few hours' notice,
bake three dozen fairy cakes,
and arrange a surprise party
with balloons.

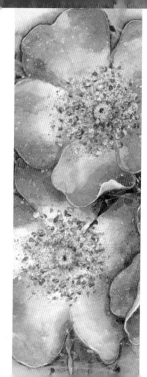

April 22

Our mother,
constant and most
certain friend.

September 12

Mothers get exasperated –
and well they might.
But they don't stop loving you.

April 23

Mothers cannot protect their children
from every sorrow, every fear,
but they can give them hope and comfort.

September 11

The family may have grown and gone – but still they are held together by memories of home.

April 24

Mothers are on standby.
Ready to pick up the pieces.
To superglue broken hearts.
To endure and forgive.

September 10

Mothers are magicians.
They can kiss away bumps and bruises.
Evict small green goblins
from the wardrobe.
Understand Jabberwocky.
Read minds. Live without sleep.

April 25

Above all else you taught me kindness –
the route to every happiness.

September 9

MOTHERS CAN MAKE
SOMETHING
OUT OF NOTHING.

April 26

Your love is the kindly fire
at which we've warmed our hands
all through our lives.

September 8

Mothers are the fulcrum on which all balances.

April 27

You have never failed us.
Never will.

September 7

The first smile. The first kiss.
The first welcome. Your mother.

April 28

We've had our differences. Skirmishes. Rows. But always, underneath the words, was the steady heartbeat of your love for me. And because of it, the temper died away and the suffering faded. And we were back together.

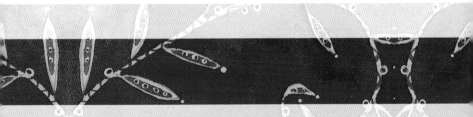

September 6

Without you, of course,
I wouldn't be here.
Without you I wouldn't have
the lovely life I have.

April 29

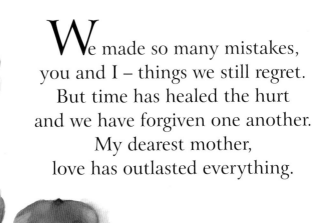

We made so many mistakes,
you and I – things we still regret.
But time has healed the hurt
and we have forgiven one another.
My dearest mother,
love has outlasted everything.

September 5

Mothers can drive
with the battle of Crécy going on
in the back of the car.

Thank you for dropping everything to get
to me in an emergency – anytime, anywhere.

April 30

Thank you for caring
about what became of me.
And making me feel
irreplaceable and loved.

September 4

Mothers come in a thousand
shapes and sizes,
softness, toughness and skills.
But one
ingredient is common
to them all. Love.

May 1

Mother Love
plumps out the
angular parts of life.

September 3

Thank you for all the small surprises,
the hugs, the smiles,
the secrets.
Thank you for giving me
the world
and teaching me
happiness.

May 2

You have loved unconditionally. Through trouble and temper, tears and sheer stupidity. Through rebellion and bouts of apathy. Through grief, bewilderment and misplaced love.

September 2

I will always keep
a little of my life set aside for you.
A place of safety.
A place of love.

May 3

The skills I have, you gave me. You hid your exasperation and smiled and said, "Let's try again." I hear you still, whatever the challenge I confront. And, failing, say, "Let's try again."

September 1

Mothers keep us safe.

May 4

You know we love you.
You know we need you.
Thank you for everything.

August 31

You were my protector –
from ghoulies and ghosties,
crocodiles and lions
under the bed.
Nothing could harm me
when you were there.

May 5

It's good when a mother and her child store things in their minds to tell each other – people they've met, things they've done, small threads that bind them together in love and understanding.

August 30

Mothers like you
have a private store of courage,
kept in reserve
to see us through even the worst
catastrophes.

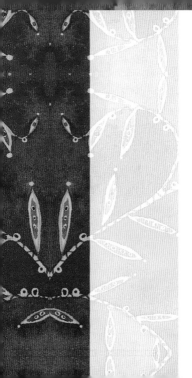

May 6

All mothers are magic
– they can run a family
and the world.

August 29

A million mothers
and each one
special.
Irreplaceable.
As you are for me.

May 7

The air is full of the telephone voices
of mothers enquiring, reminding, comforting,
scolding, encouraging, rejoicing –
webs that hold their families together.

August 28

It's only as we
grow older that
we begin to know
you as you really are –
and marvel.

May 8

We love our mothers,
hate our mothers
and finally accept
them as our friends.

August 27

Thank you for settling
for the person I turned out to be,
rather than yearning
after the person you'd rather hoped for.

May 9

There are supreme tests of endurance. Climbing Everest. Crossing the Gobi. Sailing single-handed round the world. Being a mother.

August 26

It's wonderful
to have someone
turn to you
with absolute trust....

May 10

You are a shoulder to cry on, a searcher for lost things, a provider of forgotten necessities, a waterer of plants, a booster of morale, a cheerer-on to victory. What would we do without you?

August 25

Whatever wild weather
pounds the shore
mothers stand strong – their light constant.
Their children safe.

May 11

Your hugs healed bruises, scuffs and scratches,
drove away misery, restored hope, crowned victories,
comforted a broken heart. And even now,
I feel your arms around me still,
steadying me and giving me comfort.

August 24

Motherhood is one elaborate juggling trick. Bills and fees and dashes to the doctor. Broken hearts. Broken dreams. Monumental bust-ups. And always time to listen. Always time to comfort. Always available. Night and day.

May 12

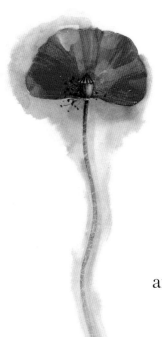

Thank you for all you were
and are and will be.
Thank you for being there
to comfort and encourage,
to share our troubled times
and our times of joy and triumph.

August 23

A mother
doesn't care what career her child
may choose –
only that it does it well, and is happy
in its choice.

May 13

"Thank you" is so inadequate. But it is all I can find to say. And that I love you.

August 22

There are mothers with the voice of angels.
Mothers who write best-selling novels.
Mothers as beautiful as any film star.
Mothers who speak five languages.
Mothers who are electricians, plumbers,
carpenters. But I much prefer you.

May 14

The pan of the scales is weighted down with responsibilities, anxieties, expenses, shattering surprises. And on the other side – a feather. Your love. And, see, the balance is perfect.

August 21

How can I thank you for
all you have given us?
Only to give my own children
the security, the encouragement, the love
you gave us, and give us still.

May 15

As long as you're
on the planet
I'm never lonely.

August 20

You held me close. You set me on my feet.
And steadied me, encouraged me,
Guided me,
Until the day you gently let go of my hands.
And let me walk alone.

May 16

You were always so astonished and delighted
when I learned to do things you had never mastered.
Ride a bike. Sail a dinghy. Drive a car.
Turn cartwheels. Thank you for your applause!
I did it for us both.

August 19

Mother Love comes swinging in when you are in trouble.

May 17

Thank you for hugs
and buttered toast,
the joys and all the small,
silly surprises
that lit my childhood.

August 18

You gave me life.
You showed me
the world.
You gave me freedom.

May 18

When I was very little I thought you perfect. When I grew older I saw, sadly, that was not so – and wished you were. But now, at long last, I love you just as you are, and you love me too.

August 17

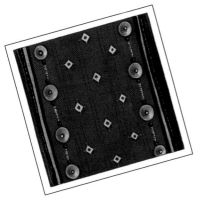

The delight
of one's mother
outweighs
any applause.

May 19

You are at the heart of all I have achieved.
Without your guidance, patience
and encouragement I could never have
found myself. I owe my life to you.

August 16

Tightening your grip to cross the road.
Such a little thing –
but living in my mind and heart forever.

May 20

Who remembers the dog licence,
the TV licence, the dentist appointment,
the optician, the magazine renewal?
Birthdays? Anniversaries? Your Mother.

August 15

Very small children
are convinced their mothers
have supernatural powers
– or at least eyes at the back
of their heads
and the ability to read minds.

May 21

Thank you for being a kooky individual as well as An Ideal Mother.

August 14

ANY JUGGLER COULD LEARN A LOT FROM ANY MOTHER.

Mothers can carry on four conversations simultaneously!

May 22

For your constancy and care when I was small.
For your patience and forgiveness.
For your sittings-up until my key was in the door.
For your faith in me. Your love for me.
For always being there for me.
Thank you, my most special mother.

August 13

I love you because you don't know everything,
because you haven't perfect self-control,
because you're rather greedy where chocolate
is concerned, because you're daft about cats,
because you always forget to shut the doors
– because you are fallible.

May 23

Mothers worry that they don't seem to fit their job description. They shouldn't worry. Their children like them as they are.

August 12

Thank you for all you did for me
when I was small.
The things I took for granted.
The things mothers do.
Nappies and sick and crying
in the night. Nose blowings,
the mopping-up of tears.
And the infinite patience
and forgiveness.

May 24

To all the mothers that hated sewing but made our costumes for the school play. To all the mothers who needed new shoes but got us ballet shoes instead. To all the mothers whose Sunday dinner consisted largely of potato doused in gravy.

August 11

MOTHERS GIVE YOU
THE GREATEST GIFT OF ALL.
LIFE ITSELF.

May 25

Your hands are strong,
capable, busy –
yet full of loving kindness
when times are hard.

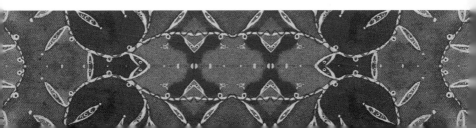

August 10

There is no section
in the Guinness Book of Records
for the number of things
a mother can do at the same time.
There should be.

May 26

Our dear mother.
The pivot about
which we turn.
The heart of
the little Universe
we call the family.

August 9

Mothers, like all good things,
are subject
to wear and tear
– but never lose their beauty
– never lose their value.

May 27

You know that compared
to most we have lived the life of royalty.
We have had time for laughter,
time for dreams. Our lives have been
rich with love.

August 8

A sunny summer day
is brighter still
if I am in your company.

May 28

Thank you for seeing us through sickness, through the griefs and the confusions of the day, for loving us and holding us together.

August 7

Nobody can divide me from my mother.
Time and distance make no difference to us.

May 29

Where there is war, where there is famine, flood or fire, there are mothers struggling to survive and bring their little ones to safety.

August 6

Mothers like you to wave
till you can't see each other any more.

May 30

When we are truly terrified
we do not call for doctors,
nurses, or the police.
We yell for our mother.

August 5

Thank you for always being ready to hop, skip, jump, throw, catch, climb, model, draw, sing, shout and applaud. It made all the difference. It made childhood a happy place to be.

May 31

Mothers turn up and lend support.
And wince at rugby tackles,
and splits and falls, missed cues
and warblings off-key.
And smile and say Well Done.
With conviction.

August 4

A mother is the one
whose face and form and scent
we can never quite remember
when we are apart –
but who lives forever
in our heart and mind.

June 1

Mothers can be out of bed
and dealing with a sick child
in two seconds flat.

August 3

A MOTHER IS BOUND
TO HER CHILDREN FOREVER
– WHATEVER MAY HAPPEN.

June 2

Thank you for being a complicated, busy, enquiring, questioning, changing human being – and not a Mother Figure.

August 2

Thank you for
my childhood
and my growing up –
for a thousand
good memories
on which I've built
my life.

June 3

Wherever we go, whatever we do,
Mum is only an arm's breadth away.

August 1

The right recipe?
The wrong recipe?
Whatever.
A mother's cooking is best.

June 4

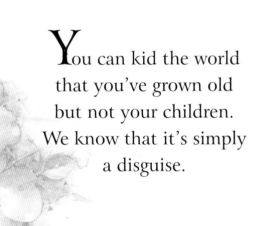

You can kid the world
that you've grown old
but not your children.
We know that it's simply
a disguise.

July 31

A dear mother.
Constancy.
Reassurance.
Comfort,
Always.

June 5

Time and again I catch myself doing things the way you did when I was small. Rubbing the leaves of the lemon balm as I pass, denting the bread rolls, folding the sheets just so.
And did your mother do it this way?
And will my children's children?

July 30

The most vital thing
we are taught by our mothers
is to love and be loved.

June 6

You are my strength, my treasure
and my friend – the rock that has endured
through all the shifting years.
My dear, my dearest mother.
Thank you.

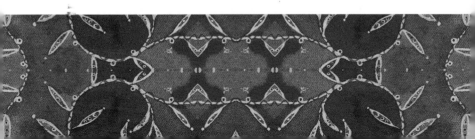

July 29

It's strange. Mothers chat and laugh with you on the telephone – but if you tell them something is most terribly wrong, suddenly they are there with you in the room.
And what seemed shapeless and overwhelming is – something you can deal with.

Mothers can do ten things at the same time. Eleven if pushed.

July 28

Thank you for saying, "Listen!"
Thank you for saying, "Look!"
Thank you for showing us the treasure
that lies inside a book.
For making every walk
an exploration, for giving us
the freedom of the sea....

Thank you for not being
the perfect mother.
None of us could have lived
up to that.
We love you exactly
as you are.

July 27

The world spins. Times change.
And yet – a mother is as much a mother
as she was five thousand years ago.
And children as loving and demanding
– and always astonishing.

You gave me life – sunshine,
starlight, oceans, forest. Friends.

July 26

Doesn't matter
where it is.
If mother
is there it's home.

June 10

It's always splendid to astonish Mum.
An outing to the bluebell woods.
A ride on the roller-coaster. A matinee.
A brand new winter coat. A bag of
Pontefract cakes. Anything
to make her smile.
As she did when we were very small.

July 25

To my dearest mother;
thank you, for finding house room
for pebbles and great chunks of rock,
for twigs and branches
and small saplings, for wriggly things
in jars, for collections of china pigs
and posters of pop idols.

June 11

Thank you for being ready
to lend anything, give anything
that will help me through.

Mothers are elasticated.
They can reach out to the edges
of the world
if their children need them.

June 12

Mothers have drawers
overflowing with scrawled letters,
postcards, paintings, things made of string
and plasticine. The jigsaw
of a family. The treasure of a lifetime.

They don't prepack love
and excitement and fun.
That comes live
from mothers like you.

June 13

Sometimes children
are swept away by circumstance –
and some seem to forget.
But at times of great trouble
they still find themselves calling
their mothers.

July 22

Thank you for sorting out the terrible Miss Smith in Infants School. Every six-year-old in the place thought you were wonderful!

June 14

People said – she's far too young
to sit through Bohème, to eat olives,
to crew a dinghy, to stand
in the snow and watch the stars fall.
You took no notice.
Thank you for being my trusting mother!

July 21

There are as many different sorts
of mother in this world as women
who have children.
How very fortunate I was to get one
who was exactly right for me.

June 15

You are my quiet place.
My haven from storm.
My shelter from harm.

July 20

There are bony mothers and fatty mothers. Mothers full of laughter and mothers full of tears. Brave mothers and mothers that would always run from a mouse. Thank you for being the best of all these things – unique and wonderful. My most special mother.

June 16

Wherever you are – in city street
or in the hush and glimmer
of a summer wood – my love is with you.
As you have always been for me.

July 19

A mother is part of a worldwide network
sharing the self same joys and sorrows.
Holding mankind together.
Understanding one another.

June 17

Some mothers and their grown-up children like to live next door to one another. Others find a gap of fifty or five hundred miles works better. Mercifully, love can stretch.

July 18

Mothers work twenty-four hours a day
seven days a week
three hundred and sixty-five days a year.
Any pay, is erratic.

June 18

Thank you for creating the scent of childhood – hot strawberry jelly, new bread, geraniums, clean sheets, lavender talc, toffee.

July 17

No mother can help it.
Nature has made her so.
She would tackle any tiger
to save her little child.
And she would still take it on
when that child is fifty.

June 19

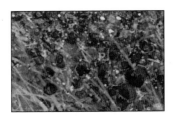

I wish everyone in the world
had a mother like you.

July 16

Without good, wise and loving mothers
the world is lost.

June 20

To my very special mother.
Thank you. Always.

July 15

A̲ny mother could set up
a business doing
Emergency Repairs of anything.

June 21

Your hands held mine
until I could walk alone.
You taught me freedom –
and when the time
had come you let me go.

July 14

Somehow, the battles are behind us. We shop together – taking delight in the sheer awfulness of much of the stuff displayed. Borrow each other's umbrellas. Are cheerfully rude to one another. Swap opinions. Even rant a little over the issues that disturb our minds. Still mother and child. But friends.

June 22

A mother can always
find time to hold you.
To talk quietly.
For just as long as you need her.

July 13

Whatever I've done
that's come right has delighted me.
And there's always a little bonus.
"My mother will be pleased."

June 23

For the smiles and frowns,
the hugs and the scoldings,
for believing in me –
even when I didn't –
A thank-you to my own
special mother.

July 12

A mother
is the lady who
for us
was never young
and will never
be old.

Every one of our achievements
is a gift to our mothers.

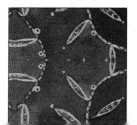

July 11

THE VERY BEST OF MOTHERS
IS YOU. KIND. PATIENT. FUNNY.
AND FULL OF LOVE.

Mothers are an
interlocking chain
that holds the world together.

July 10

I love you now and I will always love you,
whatever the future years may bring
and however times may change us.

June 26

In the wake of every evil inflicted by man or nature come the women, gathering what can be salvaged, the distraught and injured children, the lost, the dispossessed, the fragments of a broken society. They tear at blocks of stone tumbled by earthquake, blackened by fire. They build among the olive trees or the desert sand. Out of destruction they piece together small areas of safety, a home.

July 9

Thank you for making
me feel better
than I really am.

June 27

When your mother goes quiet and a little pink – she's counting to ten (or fifty if necessary).

July 8

To live fully
we need a beginning
that is love and trust
and encouragement.
Thank you....

June 28

Whenever
I don't know
where to turn –
I turn to you.

July 7

You showed me how to understand things, to read and reason and learn. You gave me such important skills.

June 29

You made me feel
wanted. Loved.
And that was the most
important thing of all.

July 6

Your mother stands
by you when
no one else will.

June 30

Thank you for
the tuckings into bed.
Thank you for the hugs
and kissings better
and all the night-time
stories that you read.

July 5

Thank you, my dearest mother,
for stars and sparrows,
for cats and carousels, for life itself.

July 1

Thank you for all the sewing-up
of rips and hanging hems, the polishing
of scuffs, the sponging-out of stains.
Thank you for all the liniment,
the sticking plasters, the linctus.
The holding of hands in thunderstorms.

July 4

Mothers have every intention of letting
you go, letting you lead your own life,
never interfering.
But they just can't help
phoning to see if
you have enough socks.
And are eating properly.

Every one of us
still lives
in our mother's love.

July 3

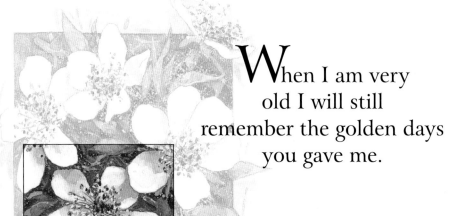

When I am very old I will still remember the golden days you gave me.